THE BE[ST]

© International Music Publications Limited
Griffin House 161 Hammersmith Road London England W6 8BS

Published 2004

New arrangements and engraving by Artemis Music Limited

Man on the Moon

Man on the Moon

If I were to pick one song as the quintessential R.E.M. song, this would be it, which is kind of ironic because it came within two hours of not being on *Automatic for the People*.

With five days left before the record was mastered, we had the track completely finished except for the lyrics. Michael was completely stumped, and was getting quite irritated with all of us leaning over his shoulder. It was decided that rather than drive each other crazy in the studio, we would take a few days off. Michael spent his time off driving around in his rental car with a cassette of the track singing along for four days.

When we reconvened, Michael walked into the studio, sang *Man on the Moon* once, and walked out. We were all stunned. It was one of those magic moments I'll remember long after the award ceremonies and photo sessions have disappeared into the mists of time.

The Great Beyond

When asked to contribute a song to the movie *Man on the Moon*, we acceded with alacrity (I just love alliteration, don't you?). Because of our love for the work of Andy Kaufman, it seemed only natural that we should write the theme song to a movie about him. The problem, of course, was that we had already written that song, namely, *Man on the Moon*. So what to do?

Rather than trying to write some kind of biography of Andy, Michael concentrated on encapsulating some of Andy's philosophy: that to keep creating you have to push forward, go beyond, attempt the impossible, in life as in art.

This is also the first song Joey Waronker played at his audition. We gave him a list of five songs to learn, and then threw a new one at him to see how quickly he thought on his feet. Very quickly, as it turns out.

Bad Day

We started writing this song in 1986. We finished writing it in 2003. The sad thing is, between those years nothing much has changed.

What's the Frequency, Kenneth?

For those who might don't know (as Mike would say), the title of this song is not original to us. Apparently in the eighties, Dan Rather, network news honcho, was assaulted by a gentleman who, between beatings, shouted "What's the frequency, Kenneth?" at him. Nobody ever figured out what that whole scene was all about.

Now let me make this completely clear: I like Dan Rather. He's a fine newsman, an interesting person to talk to, and quite a bit nuttier than most of those media types (I consider that a good thing). That said, nothing in my rich and varied life prepared me for the experience of performing behind him as he "danced" and "sang" *What's the Frequency, Kenneth?*

All The Way To Reno (You're Gonna Be A Star)

Before this had an official title, it was called "Jimmy Webb on Mars." From the six string bass intro, to the semi-rococo chord changes and through the bridge to the outro, this was musically a kind of sick tribute to a songwriter who we all admire.

Michael's lyrics add that little frisson of irony; anyone who goes to Reno to get famous is either naïve in the extreme, or seriously deluded.

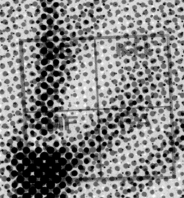

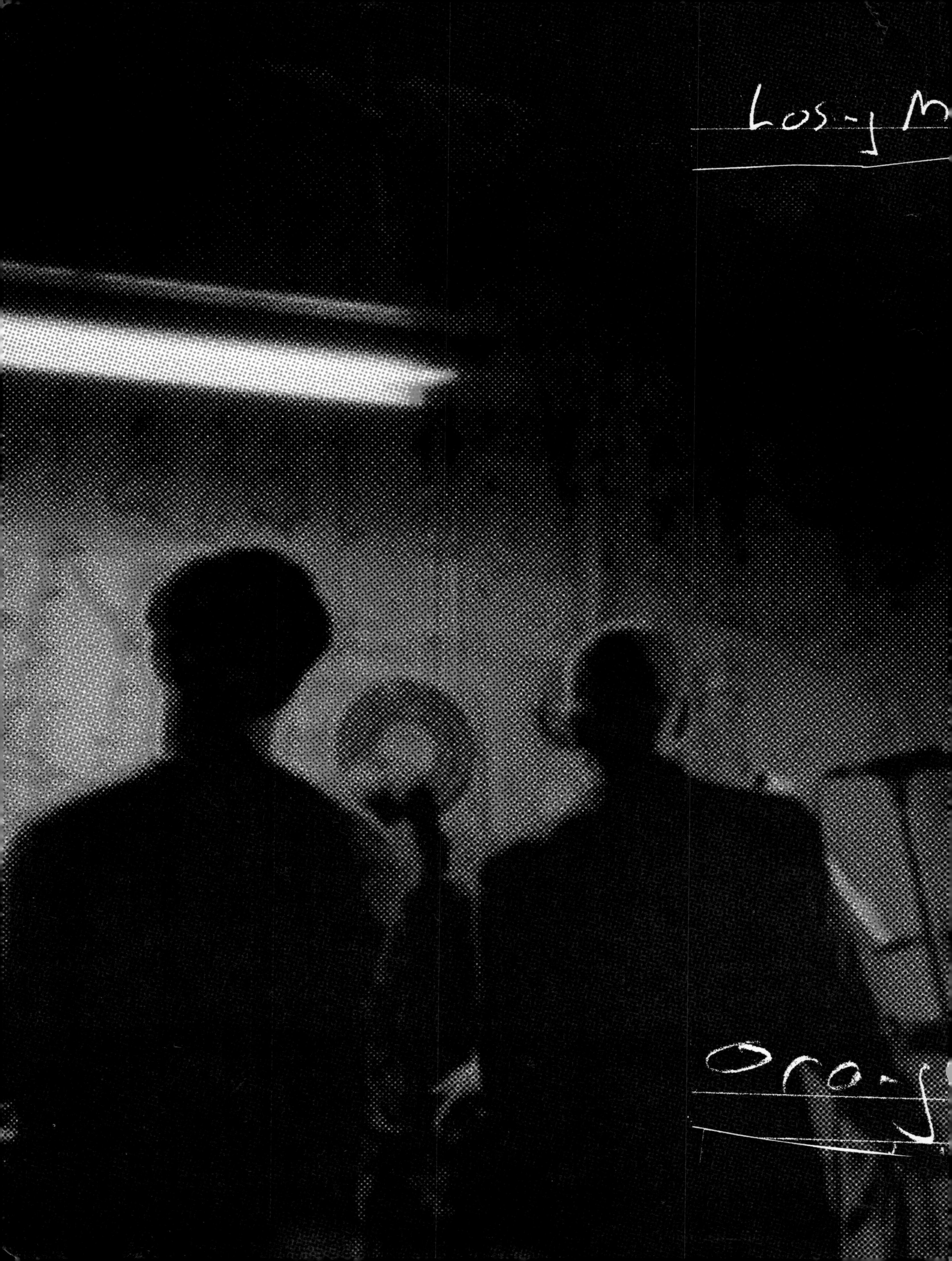

Losing My Religion

If you think about it, our career can be divided into the two parts: pre-*Losing My Religion* and post-*Losing My Religion*.

Before *Religion*, R.E.M. was a large cult band touring ten months a year. Respected and successful, we were still considered kind of minor league. Afterward, we had hit singles, platinum albums, we were on the covers of all kinds of unlikely magazines, and, at least for a couple of years, were one of the biggest bands in the world. All of which is irrelevant.

When I think about *Losing My Religion*, I think about the process of writing and recording it, and how dream-like and effortless it was. The music was written in five minutes; the first time the band played it, it fell into place perfectly. Michael had lyrics within the hour, and while playing the song for the third or fourth time, I found myself incredibly moved to hear the vocals in conjunction with the music. To me, *Losing My Religion* feels like some kind of archetype that was floating around in space that we managed to lasso. If only all songwriting was this easy.

E-Bow the Letter

I first saw Patti Smith perform in 1976, and I remember thinking that I would gladly give ten years off my life to be the bass player for her group. I know Michael was equally as inspired by Patti, and when he came up with a Ronettes style vocal chorus, it was obvious who we had to call.

It was such an incredible experience watching Patti sing this song–a song we wrote! I had all the cliché reactions: chills ran up and down my spine, the hair stood up on the back of my neck, etc. My life did not flash before my eyes, but it was a close thing.

When the session was over, I walked out into the night high as a kite, completely transported.

Orange Crush

I must have played this song onstage over three hundred times, and I still don't know what the fuck it's about. The funny thing is, every time I play it, it means something different to me, and I find myself moved emotionally.

Noel Coward made some remark about the potency of cheap music, and while I wouldn't describe this song as cheap in any way, sometimes great songwriting isn't the point. A couple of chords, a good melody, and some words can mean more than a seven hundred-page novel. Not a good seven hundred page novel mind you, but more than say, a long Jacqueline Susan novel. Well, alright, I really liked <u>Valley of the Dolls</u>.

I guess I've found a good way not to talk about a song that means something dark and mysterious to me.

Selah.

Imitation of Life

This song was the poppiest thing on *Reveal*, and hence the first single. The title, of course, comes from the Douglas Sirk film about an African-American woman passing for white in the south in the fifties, a movie which I don't think any of us have actually seen.

I thought at the time that the title was a perfect metaphor for adolescence. Unfortunately, I've come to believe that it is a perfect metaphor for adulthood, too. But that's another story.

Funnily enough, we had written, recorded, and released this song before I realized that the first four chords in the verse are the exact same chords as the verse of *Driver 8*. Oh well.

Daysleeper

On an album (*Up*) not exactly chock-full of top pop smashes, this was the first single. Although not at all representative of the album, I've always liked this song. After all, when was the last time that a song in 3/4 time was a hit single?

Lyrically, what can I say? I relate. After all the years we've been a band, the one thing I know we have in common is that we stay up all night and sleep in the day. Also, we're all incredibly stubborn, so I guess that's two things. Anyway, I think this song perfectly captures that woozy, seasick feeling you get during the daylight hours when you haven't slept.

Animal

Animal

This is the newest song on the record. It is also the most spontaneous. It was recorded in about fifteen minutes. Within a couple of weeks from first hearing it, Michael had written and sung the vocals (including that creepy robot backing vocal). Mike then put on his Arabic-type vocal, I added lead guitar, and it was finished. Now all I have to do is convince the guys that everything should be done this quickly. Who knows? It could happen.

Sidewinder Sleeps Tonite

The Sidewinder Sleeps Tonite

We included this song on *Automatic* in order to break the prevailing mood of the album. Given that lyrically the record dealt with mortality, the passage of time, suicide and family, we felt that a light spot was needed. In retrospect, the consensus among the band is that this might be a little too lightweight.

Stand

Stand

Without a doubt, *Stand* is the, um, how shall I put this? It's the stupidest song we've ever written. That's not necessarily a bad thing though. A lot of my favorite rock and roll records have been extravagantly dumb, and while *Stand* doesn't reach the god-like heights of inspired stupidity as a song like *Louie Louie* by The Kingsmen does, we're at least playing in the same ballpark.

The listener might want to note the guitar solo; I'd just bought a wah-wah pedal that morning. The first thing I used it on was the solo on *Stand*. When I looked around to see what everyone thought, I was met with gales of uncontrollable laughter. I assumed that anything that could inspire that kind of reaction must be good. I hope I was right.

Electrolite

Electrolite

I love this song. The track was recorded somewhere in Arizona on the 1995 tour at soundcheck and finished in Seattle in 1996. It's probably the least melodramatic pre-millennial folk-blues end of the century good-bye song ever written. It might also be the only one, but whatever.

My only complaint? When we play this song live, I get saddled with playing the god damned banjo. The thing weighs ninety pounds and has strings made of the same stuff they use on cheese slicers. Talk about suffering for your art! Well, it may not exactly be art, and I don't really suffer, but I'm sure you get the drift.

All the Right Friends

This is by far the oldest song on this set. It was written in 1979 by Michael and me before we had ever met Bill and Mike. We played it at every show until about 1982. I don't know why we never recorded it; maybe we thought it was kind of juvenile.

Twenty years later, when asked to contribute a song to the *Vanilla Sky* soundtrack with about eight days notice, it no longer seemed quite so naïve. We recorded it in three hours prior to a show in Seattle, and quite consciously tried to approach it as we would have in 1982.

All the right friends

Everybody hurts

Everybody Hurts

This song doesn't really belong to us anymore; it belongs to everybody who has ever gotten any solace from it. The reason that the lyrics are so atypically straightforward is because it was aimed at teen-agers. I've never watched Buffy the Vampire Slayer, but the idea that high school is a portal to hell seems pretty realistic to me. It's hard for everyone.

Musically, Bill Berry originated the chord changes, and after a couple of weeks of arrangement hell, we settled on an Otis Redding type vibe. Thanks Steve Cropper.

At My Most Beautiful

At My Most Beautiful

Obviously, this is our tribute to the Beach Boys. Mike told me that when he and Bill lived in Macon, they would cruise the city, singing along with a Beach Boys eight-track. He said it really stretched their upper ranges. Until the day Bill quit, they could both still hit those notes.

I'm not sure that Michael even knows that the Beach Boys have an un-released album called Smile, but he went along with the feel of the track, knowing that Mike and I are big fans.

The bass part on this is probably my favorite line that Mike has ever come up with. When we play it live, I play bass. I feel like such a pro, up on stage playing this super cool part.

Nightswimming

Nightswimming

Nightswimming is the only song we've ever written where the words came first. During the mixing stage of Out of Time, Michael came to us with a complete set of lyrics and suggested that we might want to put them to music. Being the competitive bastards that we are, Mike and I started auditioning chord changes and tunes for Michael. The two tunes of mine that Michael rejected eventually became Drive and Try Not to Breathe. Mike had a piano instrumental that he played to Michael. He listened once, nodded his head to hear it again, and on the second pass he sang the lyrics. It was Nightswimming, exactly like the record we would record a year later. I was standing in the corner, dumbfounded.

- Peter Buck

MAN ON THE MOON

Words and Music by William Berry, Peter Buck, Michael Mills and Michael Stipe

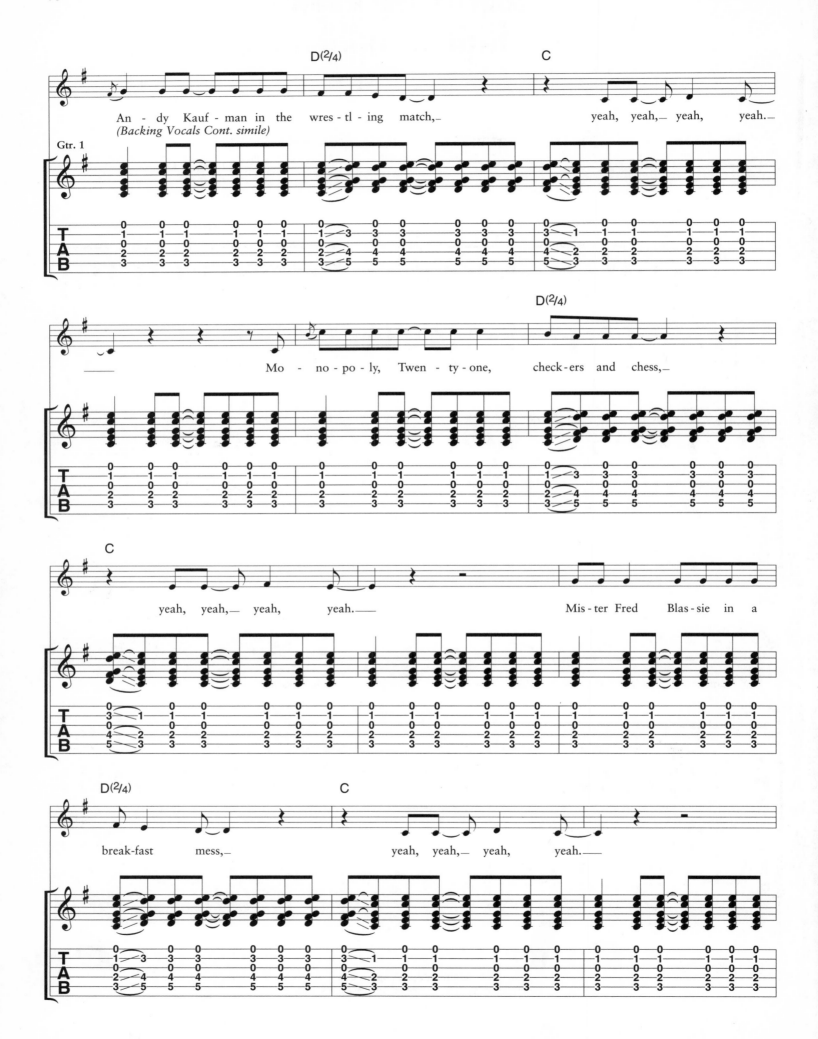

Hey An-dy, are you goof-ing on El - vis? Hey ba-by,

are we los-ing touch?

end Fig. 3

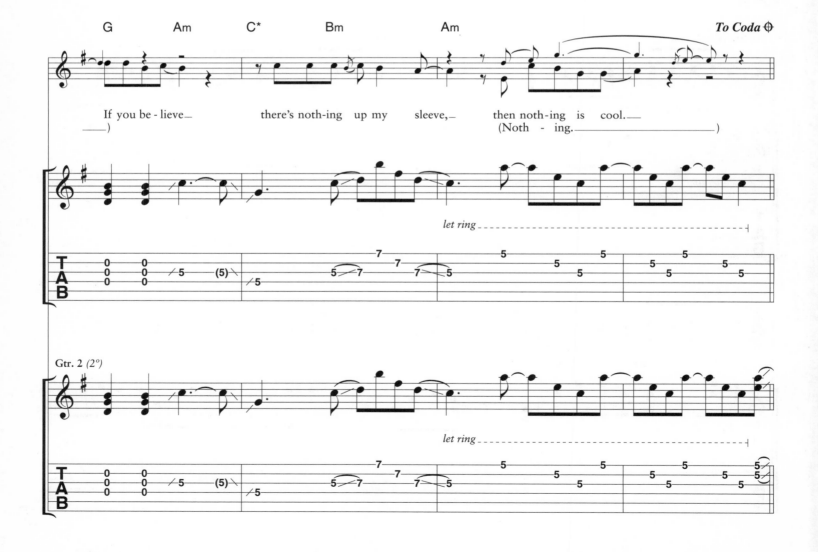

are   we   los - ing   touch?____

Chorus: G   Am   C*   Bm   G   Am

If you be - lieved   they put a man on the moon,   man on the moon.
(w/background Fig. 1)

Gtr. 2

w/Fig. 4 (Acous. Gtr. 3) 3 times   *let ring*   *let ring*

D   G   Am   C*   Bm

(Doo - ah,   doo - ah, ah doo.)   If you be - lieve   there's noth - ing up my   sleeve,

Am

then noth - ing is cool.
(Noth - ing.)

let ring

Background Vocal Fig. 1

Man   on the moon.

THE GR EAT BEYOND

Words and Music by Peter Buck, Michael Mills and Michael Stipe

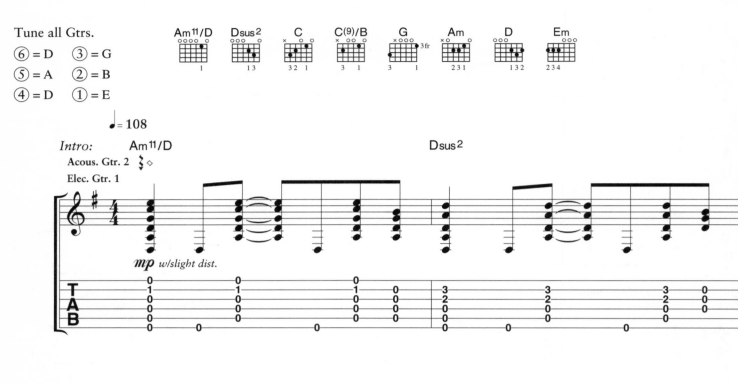

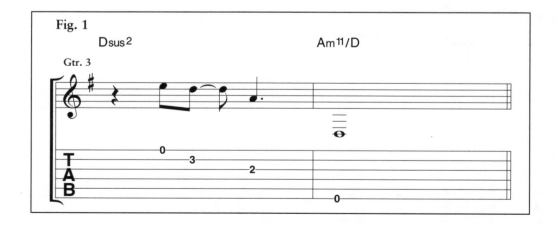

Fig. 1

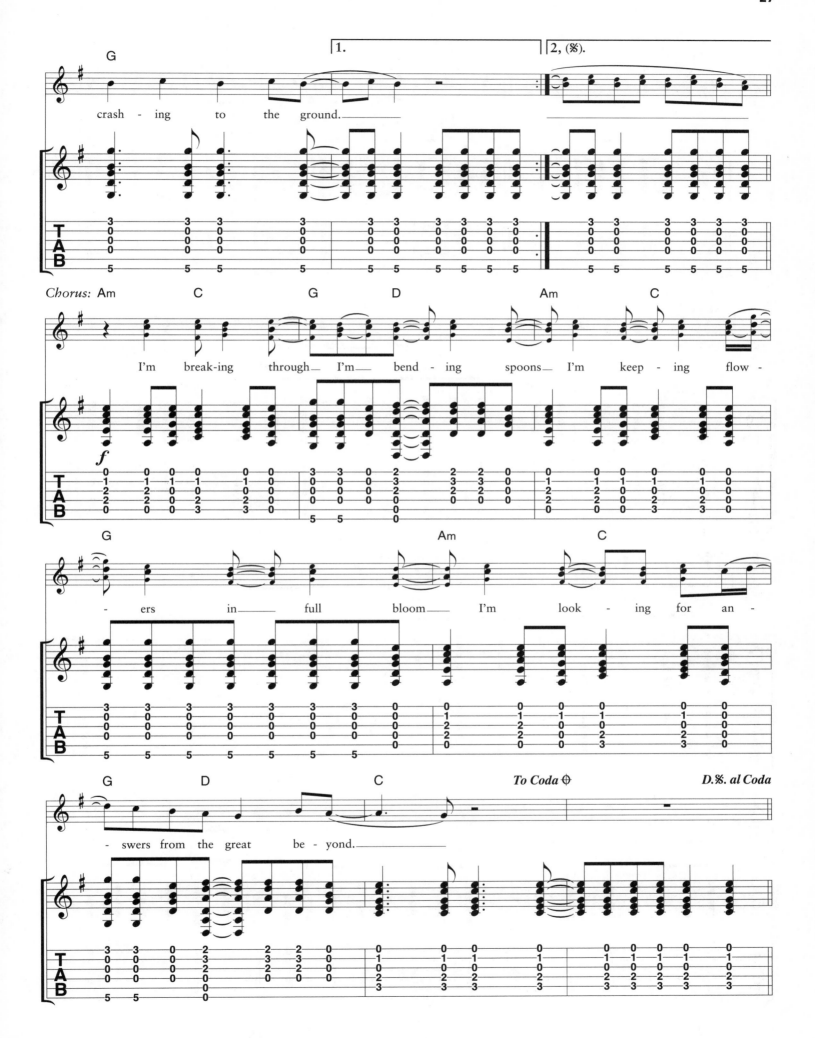

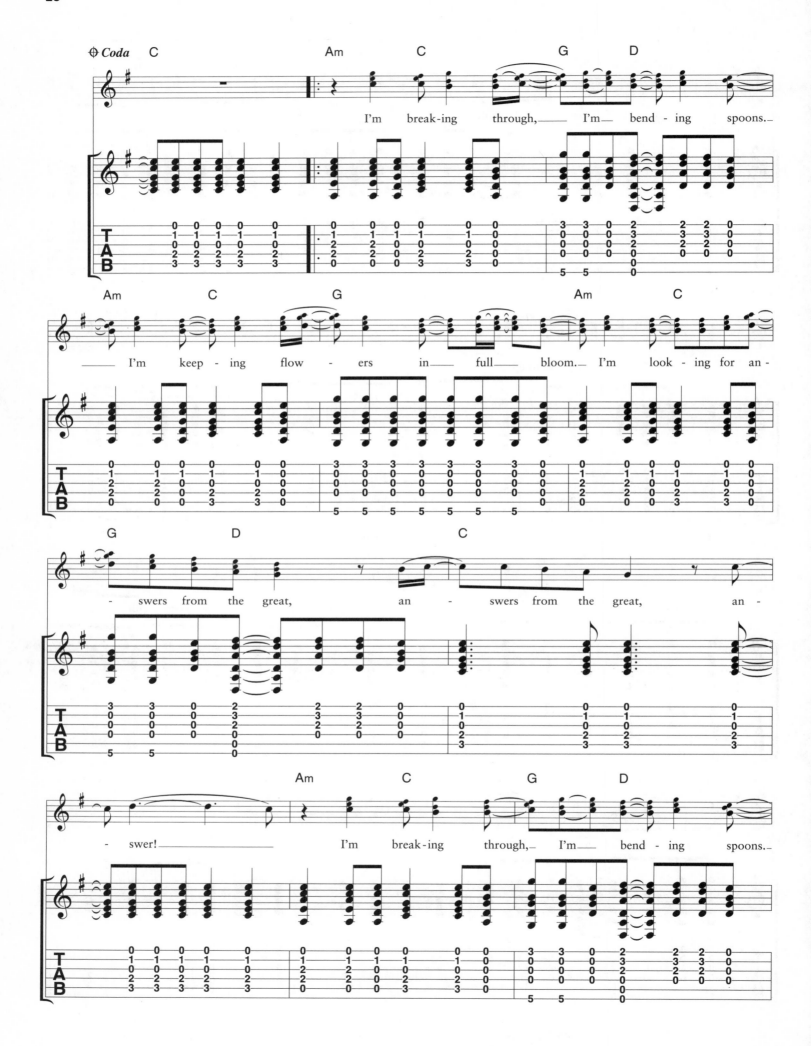

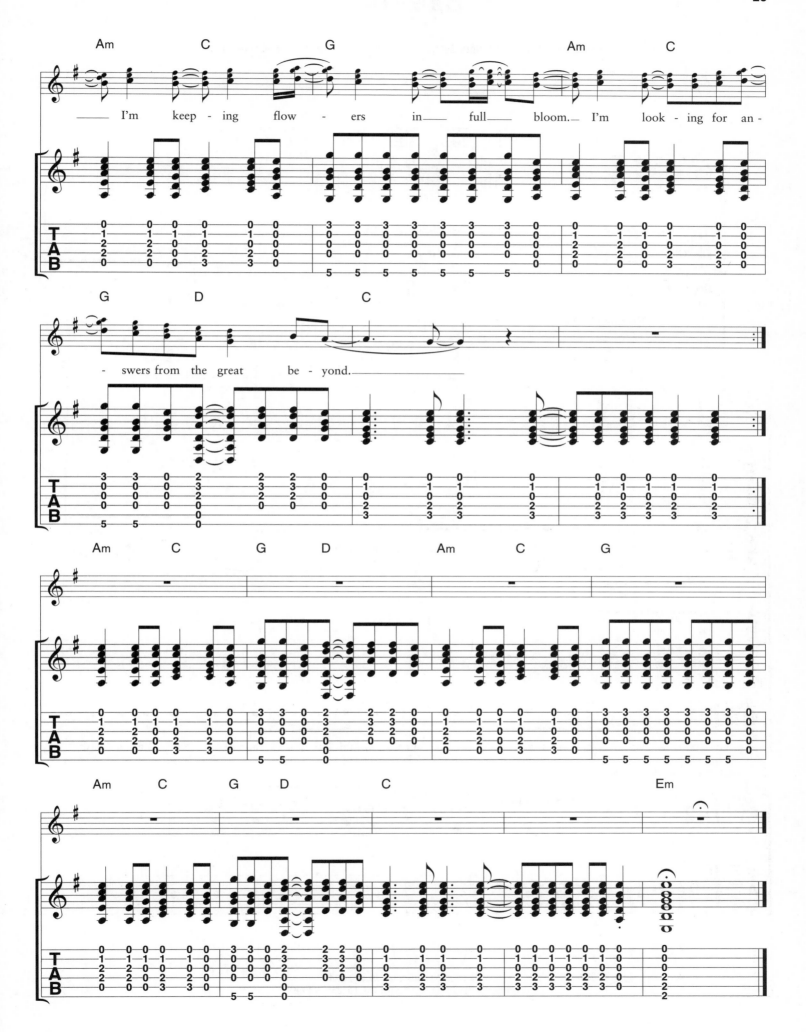

BAD DAY

Words and Music by William Berry, Peter Buck, Michael Mills and Michael Stipe

mit - tee prize in - ves - ti - ga - tion dance? Those

I____ paid it nev - er mind,____

go a - way.
ants - in - pants glan - ces. Well look be - hind____ the eyes____

Shit's so thick____ you could stir____

w/Fig. 1 *(Elec. Gtr. 1)*   end Fig. 3

____ with a stick,____ free.
____ it's a

Tef - lon, white - washed pre - si - den - cy.____ We're
hal - lowed, hol - low a - naes - the - tized____

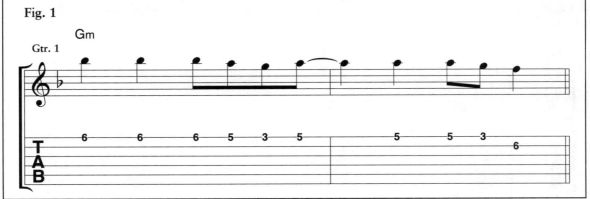

Fig. 1

Gtr. 1   Gm

Fig. 2

Du du du, du du du. I

saw that I keep be-hind.

Du du du, du du du. D.%%. al Coda ⊕⊕

⊕⊕ *Coda*

Chorus:

It's been a bad day, please don't take

Gtrs. 3 & 4

Gtr. 3

Gtr. 2

Gtr. 4

w/Fig. 4 *(Elec. Gtr. 2) 4 times*

Verse 3:
We're dug in deep, the price is steep.
The auctioneer is such a creep.
The lights went out, the oil ran dry
We blamed it on the other guy.
Sure, all men are created equal.
Here's the church, here's the steeple.
Please stay tuned, we cut to sequel.
Ashes, ashes, we all fall down.

Broadcast me a joyful noise unto the times, lord.
Count your blessings,
Ignore the lower fear
Ugh, this means war,

It's been a bad day *etc.*

WHAT'S THE FREQUENCY, KENNETH?

Words and Music by William Berry, Peter Buck, Michael Mills and Michael Stipe

I was brain-dead, locked out, numb, not up to speed.
Richard said, "With-drawal in dis - gust is not the same as a - pa - thy."

2, 3. A

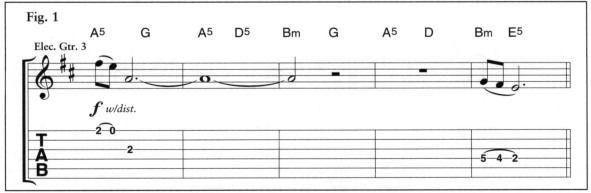

Fig. 1

Pre-chorus:

(1.) I thought I'd pegged you, an i - di - ot's dream.__
smile like the car - toon, tooth for a tooth,__

Tun - nel vi - sion from the out - si - der's screen.__
you said that i - ro - ny was the shack - les of youth.__

Chorus:

I nev - er un - der-stood the fre - quen - cy, uh - huh.
You wore a shirt_____ of vi - o - lent green, uh - huh.

w/Fig. 2 *(Elec. Gtr. 2) 4 times*

Fig. 2

Elec. Gtr. 2

w/tremolo

You wore our ex - pec - ta - tions like an ar - mored suit, uh - huh.
I nev - er un - der - stood the fre - quen - cy, uh - huh.

You wore our ex - pec - ta - tions like an ar - mored suit, uh - huh.
You wore a shirt of vi - o - lent green, uh - huh.

Verse 3:
"What's the frequency, Kenneth?"
Is your Benzedrine, uh-huh.
Butterfly decal, rear-view mirror
Dogging the scene.

You smile like a cartoon *etc.*

All The Way To Reno

Words and Music by Peter Buck, Michael Mills and Michael Stipe

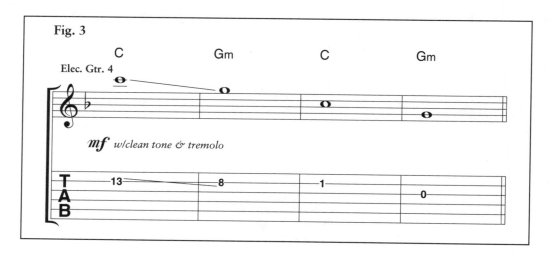

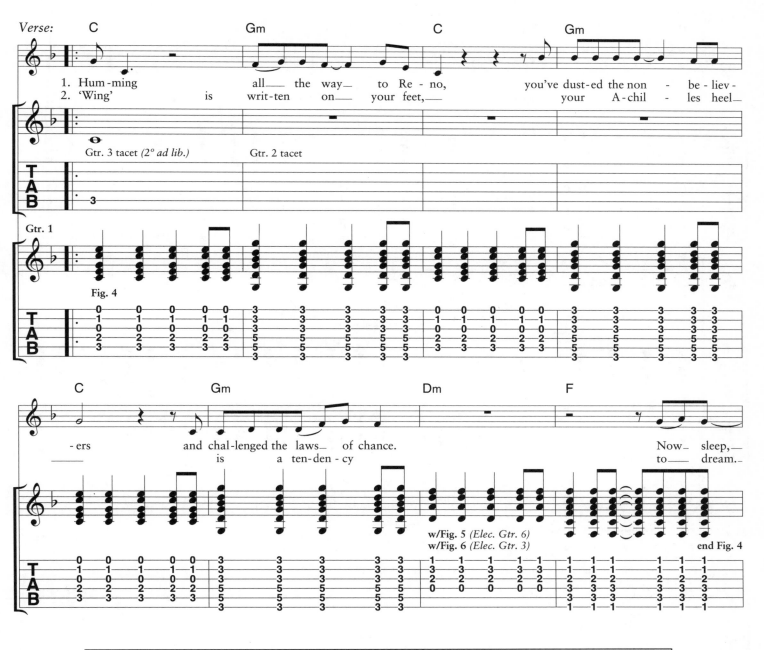

Verse:

1. Hum-ming all the way to Re - no, you've dust-ed the non - be - liev-ers
2. 'Wing' is writ-ten on your feet, your A-chil - les heel is a ten-den - cy

Gtr. 3 tacet (2° ad lib.) Gtr. 2 tacet

Gtr. 1

Fig. 4

and chal-lenged the laws of chance. Now sleep, to dream.

w/Fig. 5 (Elec. Gtr. 6)
w/Fig. 6 (Elec. Gtr. 3)
end Fig. 4

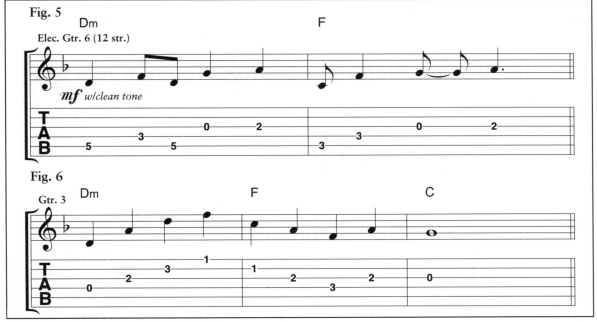

Fig. 5

Dm   F

Elec. Gtr. 6 (12 str.)

mf w/clean tone

Fig. 6

Gtr. 3   Dm   F   C

You know what you are,—— you're gon - na be a star.——

To Coda ⊕ | 1. | 2.

end Fig. 8

end Fig. 9

Bridge: Dm   Gm   Dm   Gm

(Gtr. 1)   *Cont. rhy. simile*

You__ know__ who__ you are,_____ you__ know__ who__ you __ are,_____

Gtrs. 3 & 4

48

you— know— who— you are._____

Interlude:

w/Fig. 1 *(Elec. Gtr. 2) 2 times*
w/Fig. 2 *(Elec. Gtr. 3) 2 times*
w/Fig. 3 *(Elec. Gtr. 4)*
Gtr. 5 plays ad lib. w/backwards fx

Verse:

Hum-ming   all— the way— to Re-no,   you've writ-ten your own— di-rec-

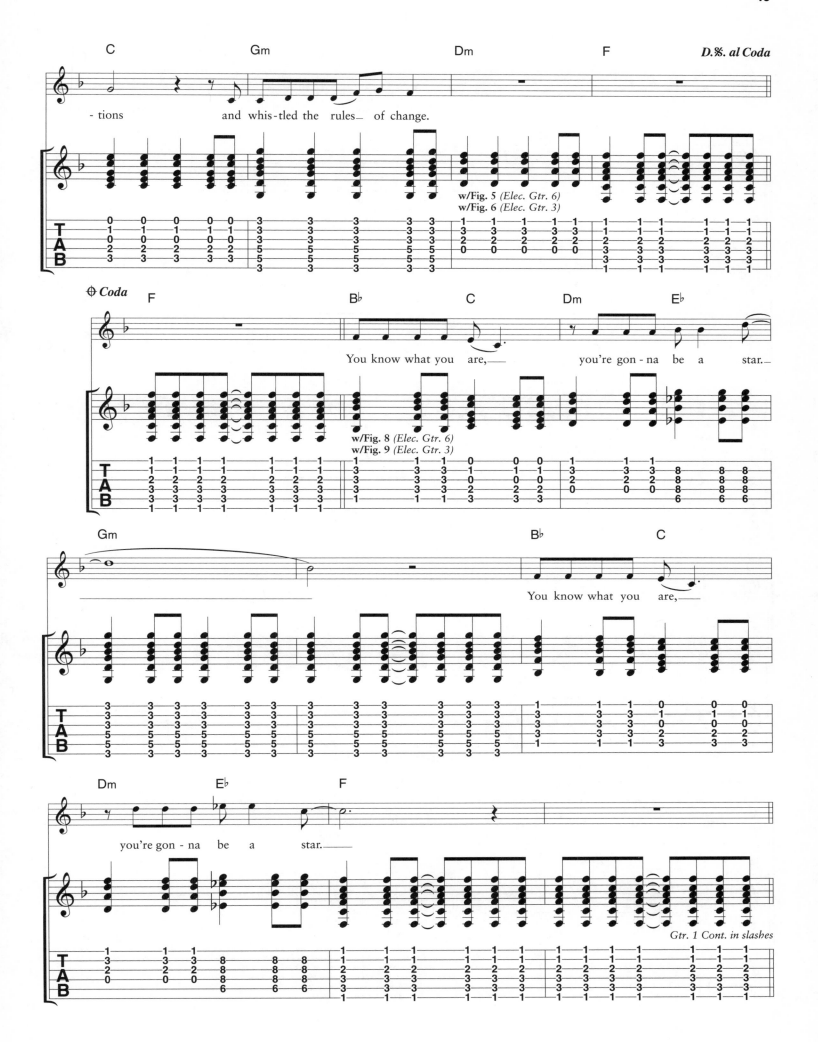

You know what you are, you're gon-na be a star.

LOSING MY RELIGION

Words and Music by William Berry, Peter Buck, Michael Mills and Michael Stipe

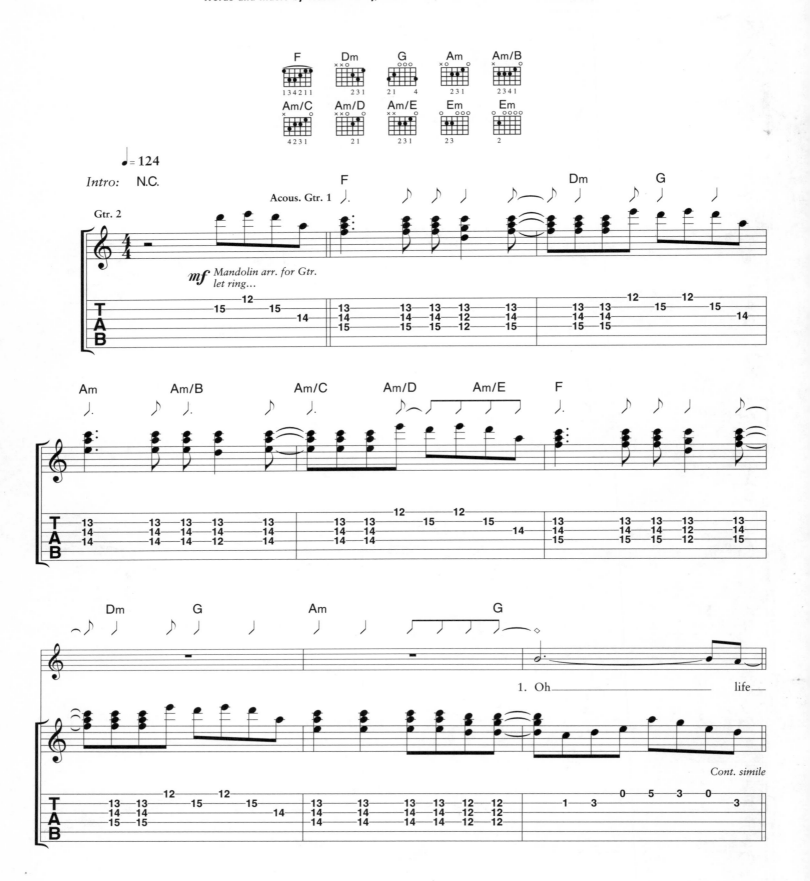

1. Oh_____ life____

Cont. simile

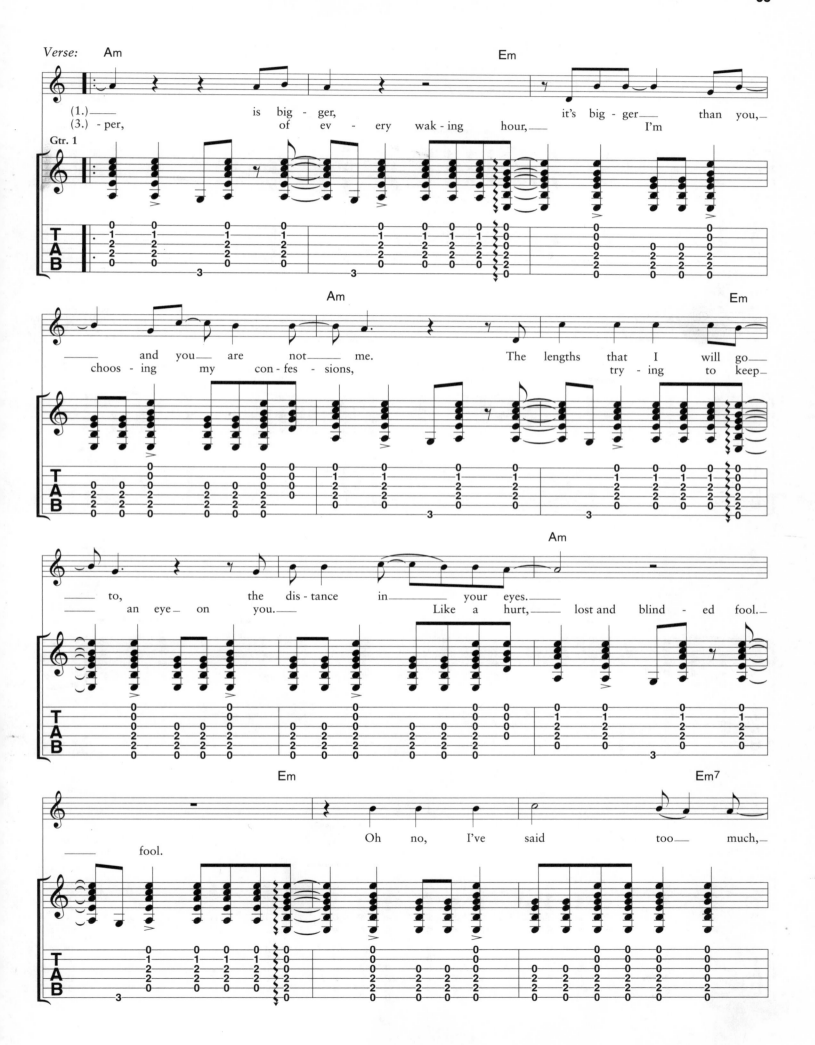

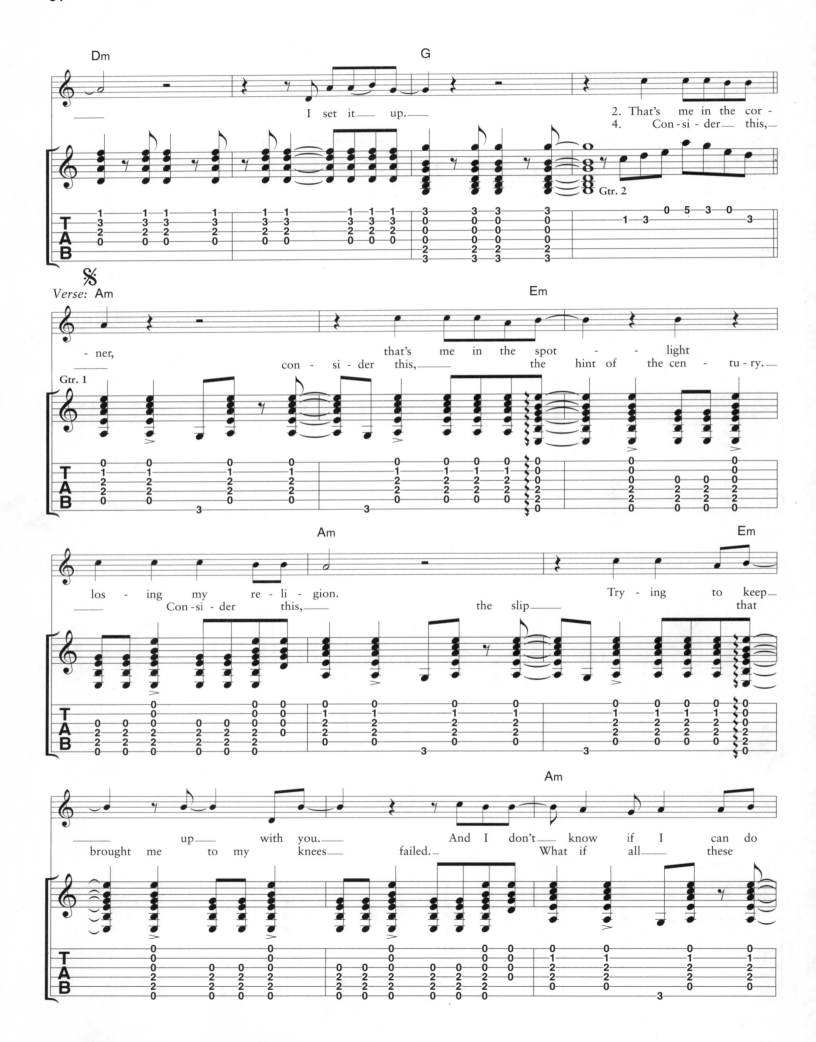

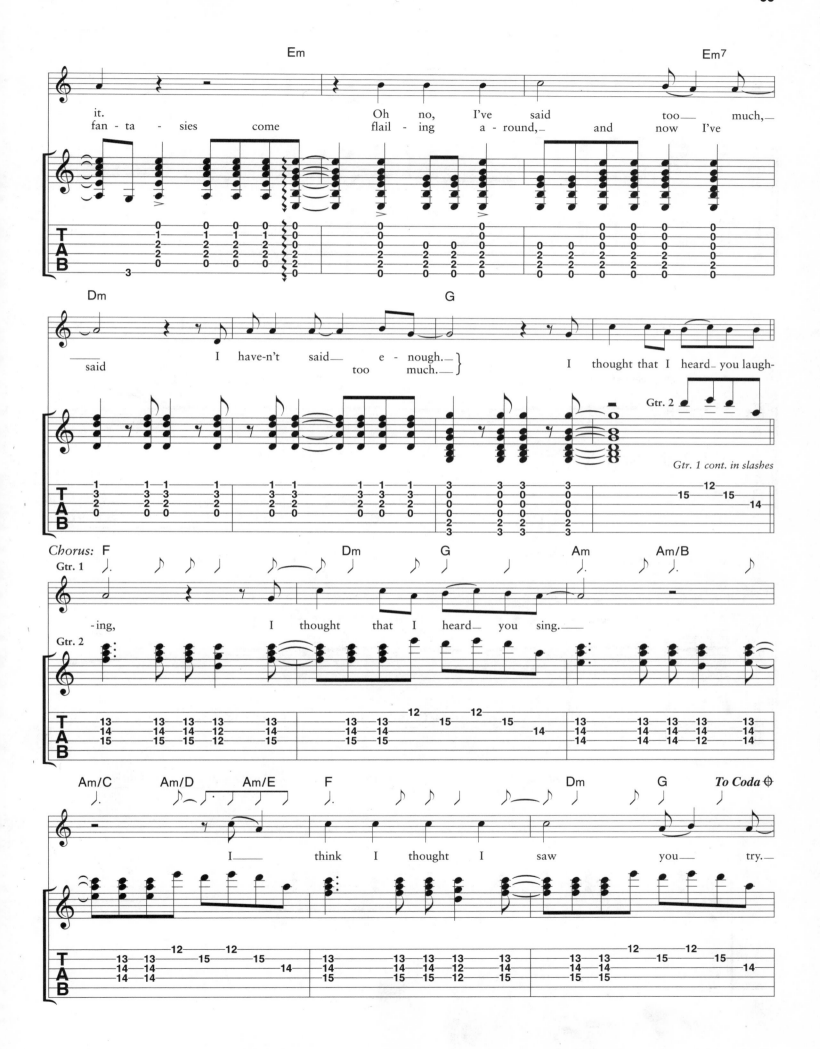

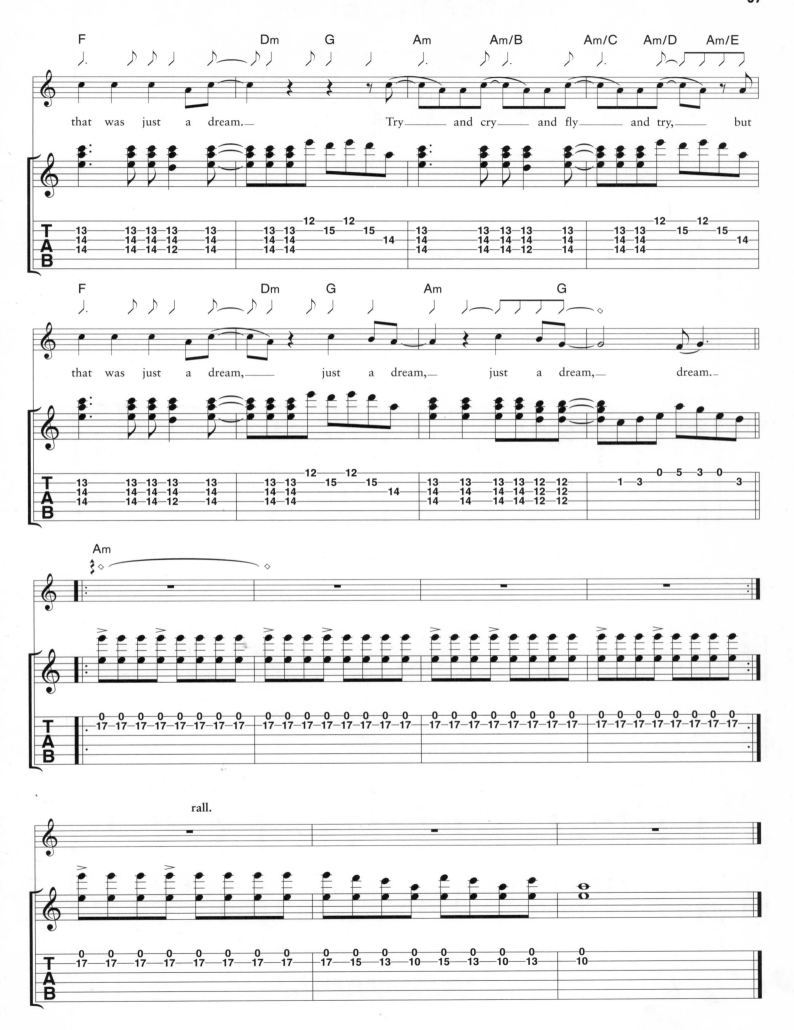

E-BOW THE LETTER

Words and Music by William Berry, Peter Buck, Michael Mills and Michael Stipe

Fig. 2

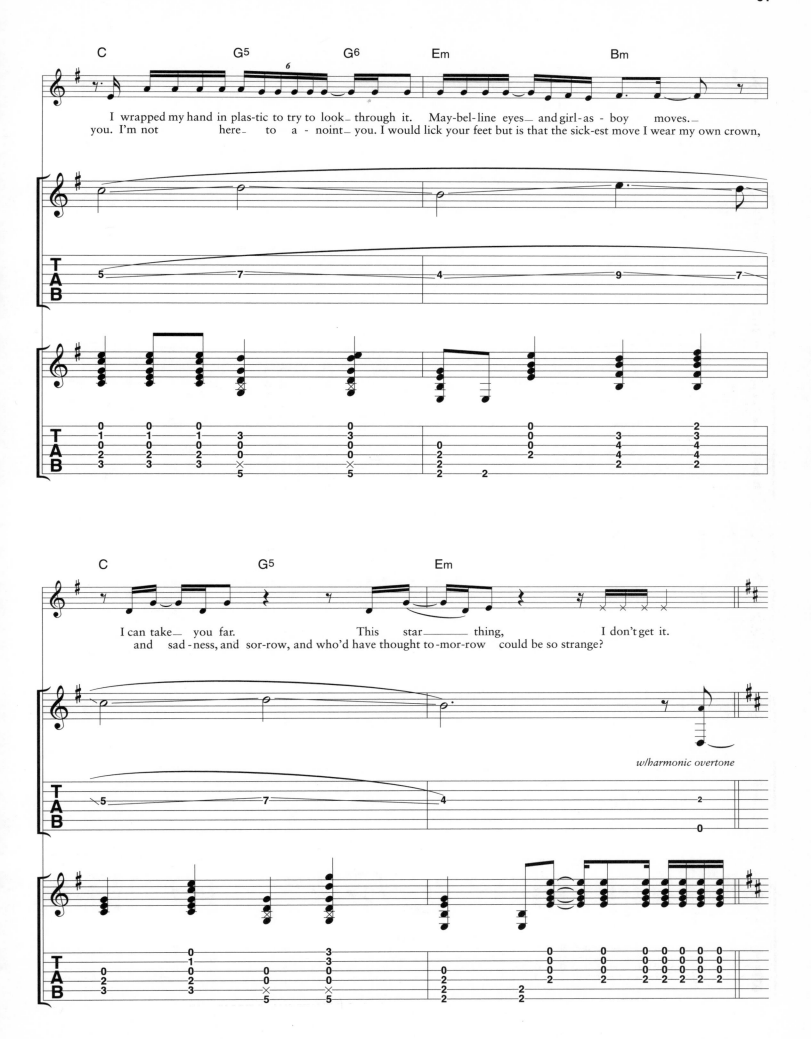

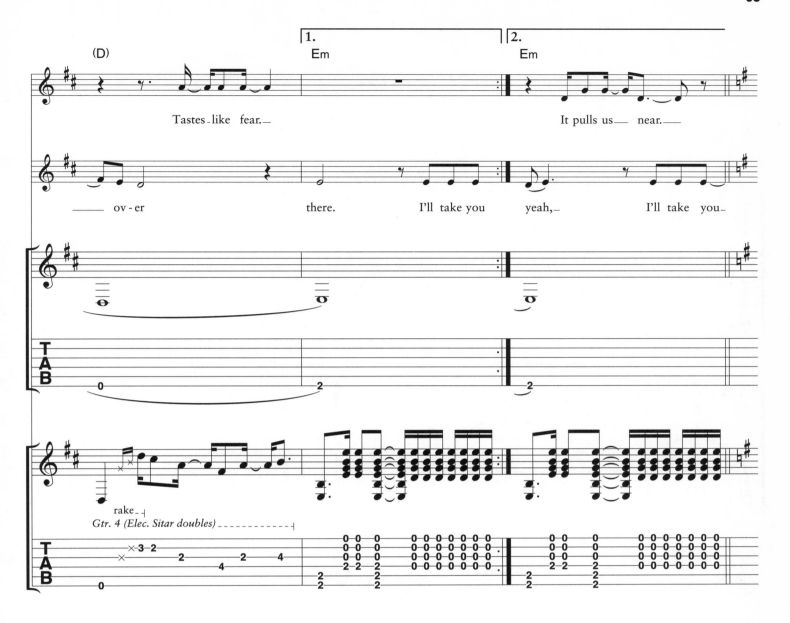

Interlude:

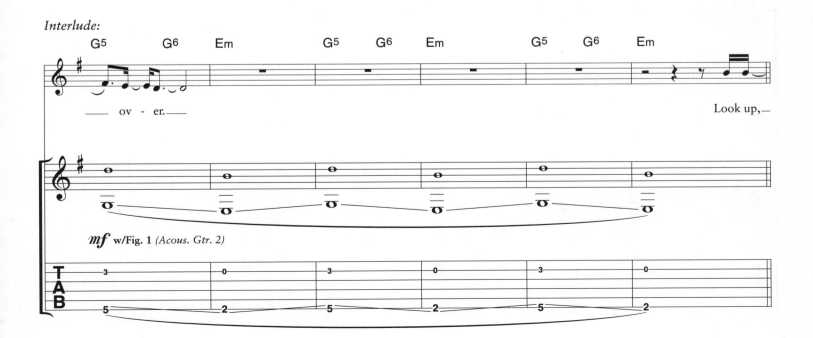

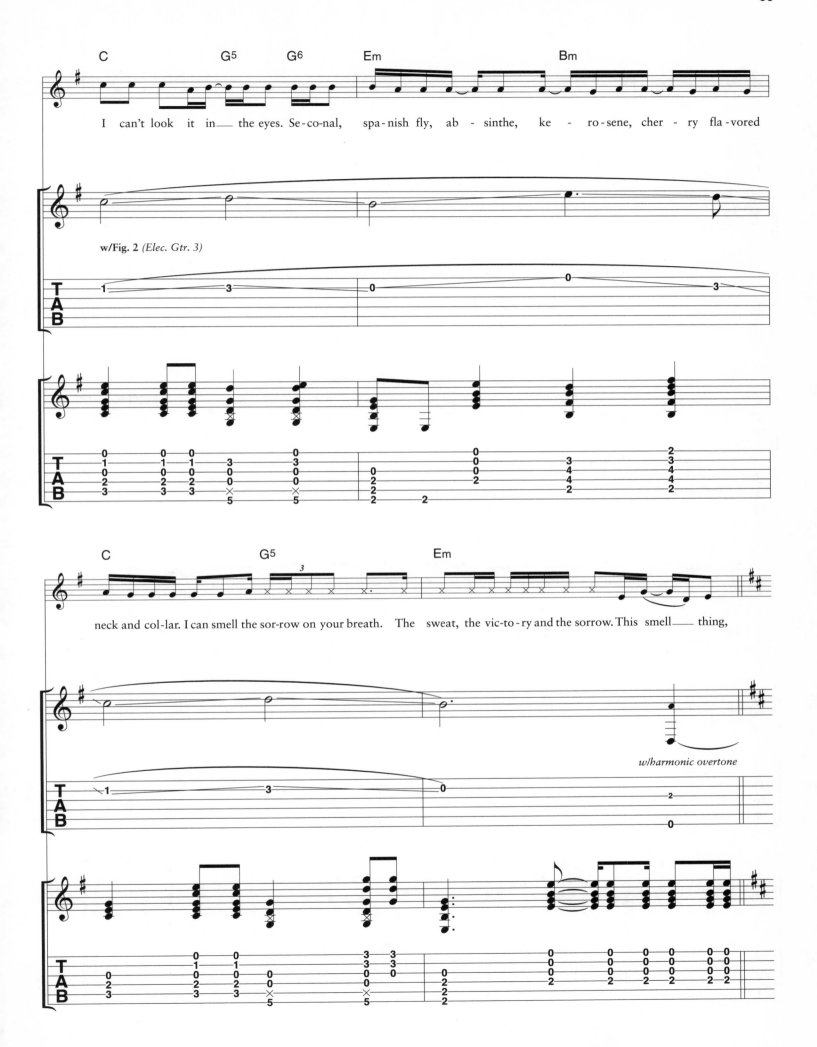

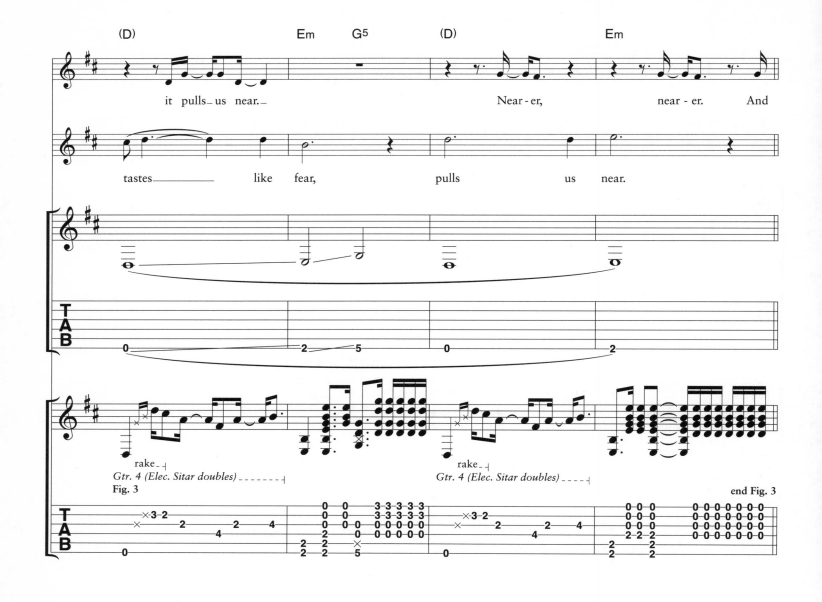

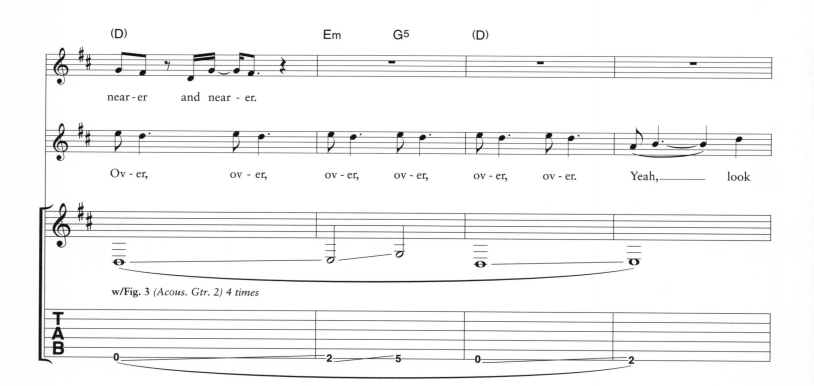

ORANGE CRUSH

Words and Music by William Berry, Peter Buck, Michael Mills and Michael Stipe

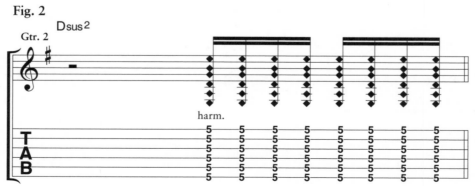

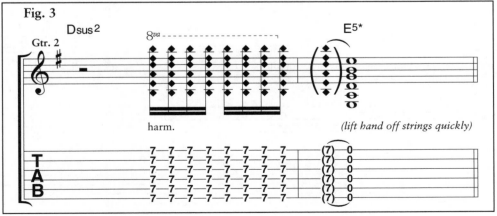

Fig. 3

IMITATION OF LIFE

Words and Music by Peter Buck, Michael Mills and Michael Stipe

su - gar - cane— that tast-ed good,— that's who you are,— that's

what you could,— come on,— come on,— no one— can see— you cry.—

That

DAYSLEEPER

Words and Music by Peter Buck, Michael Mills and Michael Stipe

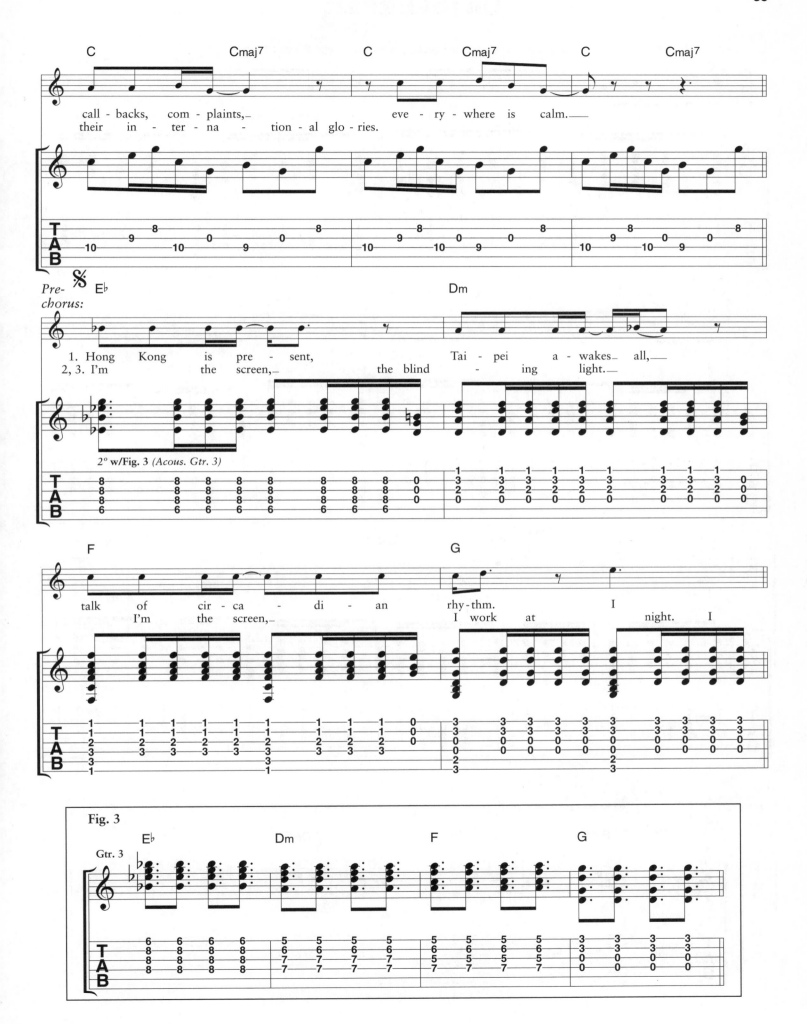

Fig. 3

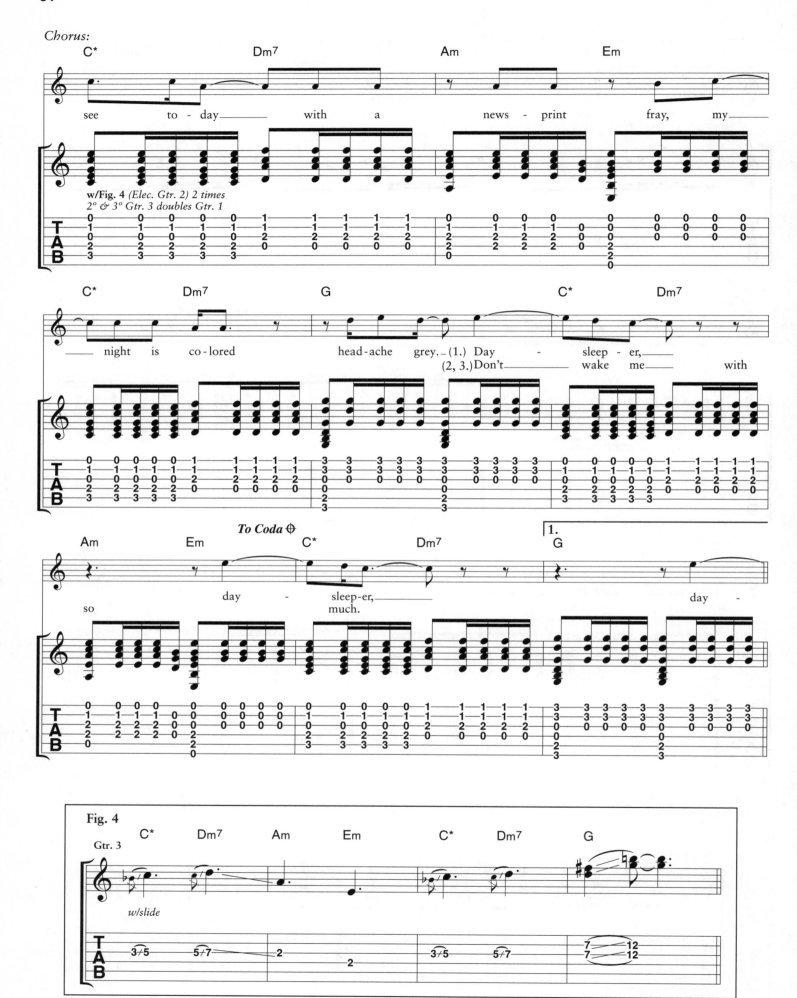

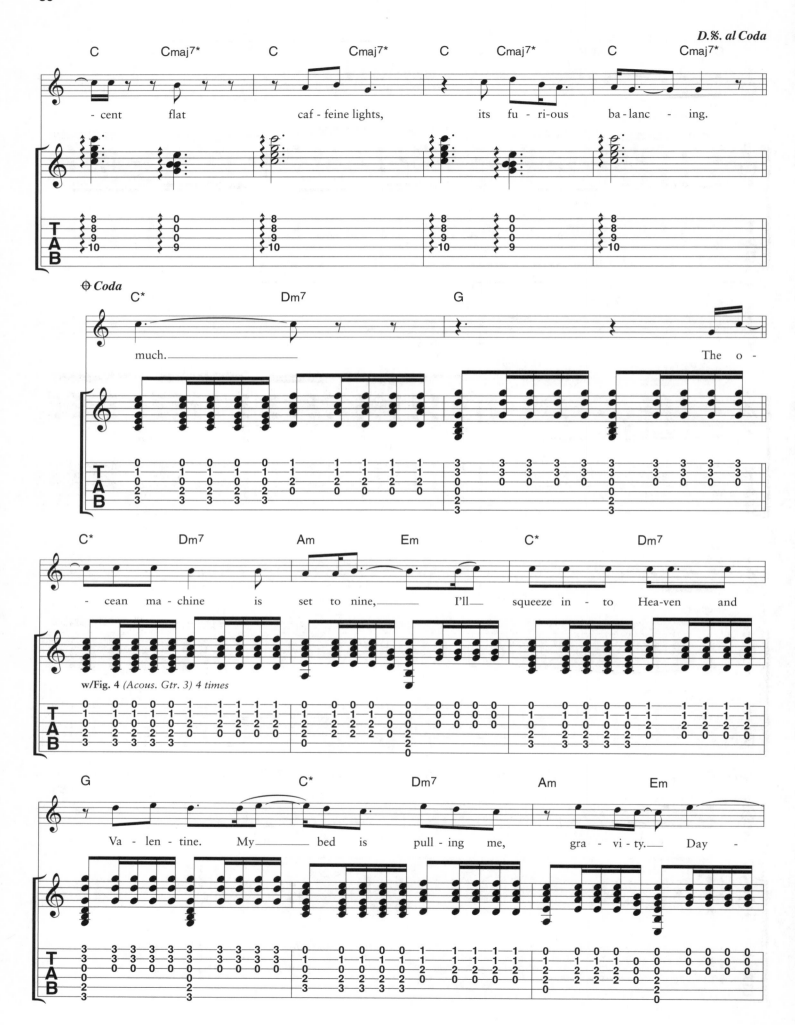

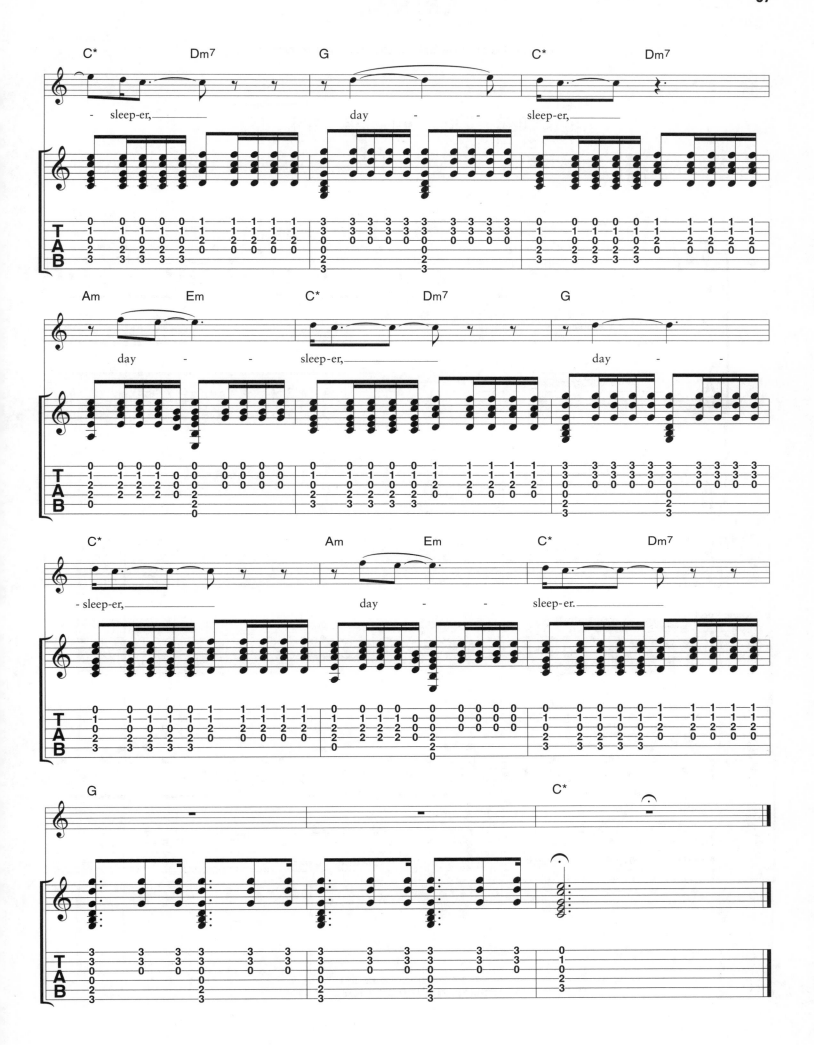

ANIMAL

Words and Music by Peter Buck, Michael Mills and Michael Stipe

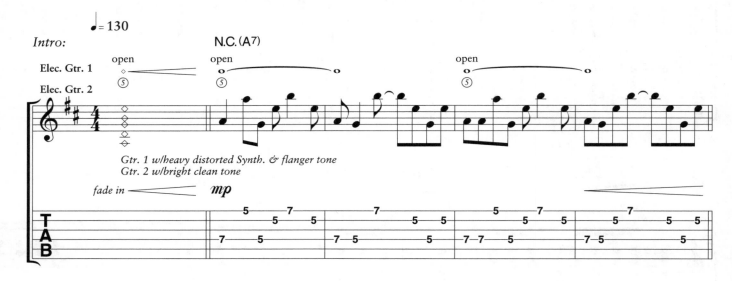

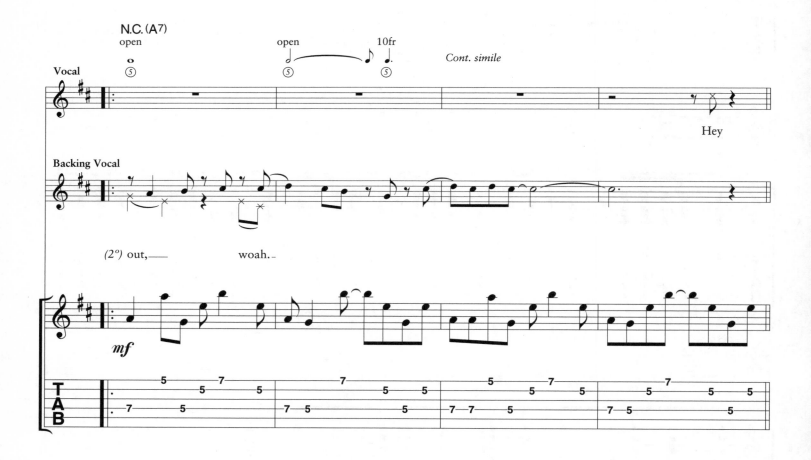

Verse 3:
I am vibrating at the speed of light
Take my hand, we'll wind up the night.
Spin me, win me, lift me, kiss me
Trip me, cuss me, bend me, trust me.

THE SIDEWINDER SLEEPS TONITE

Words and Music by William Berry, Peter Buck, Michael Mills and Michael Stipe

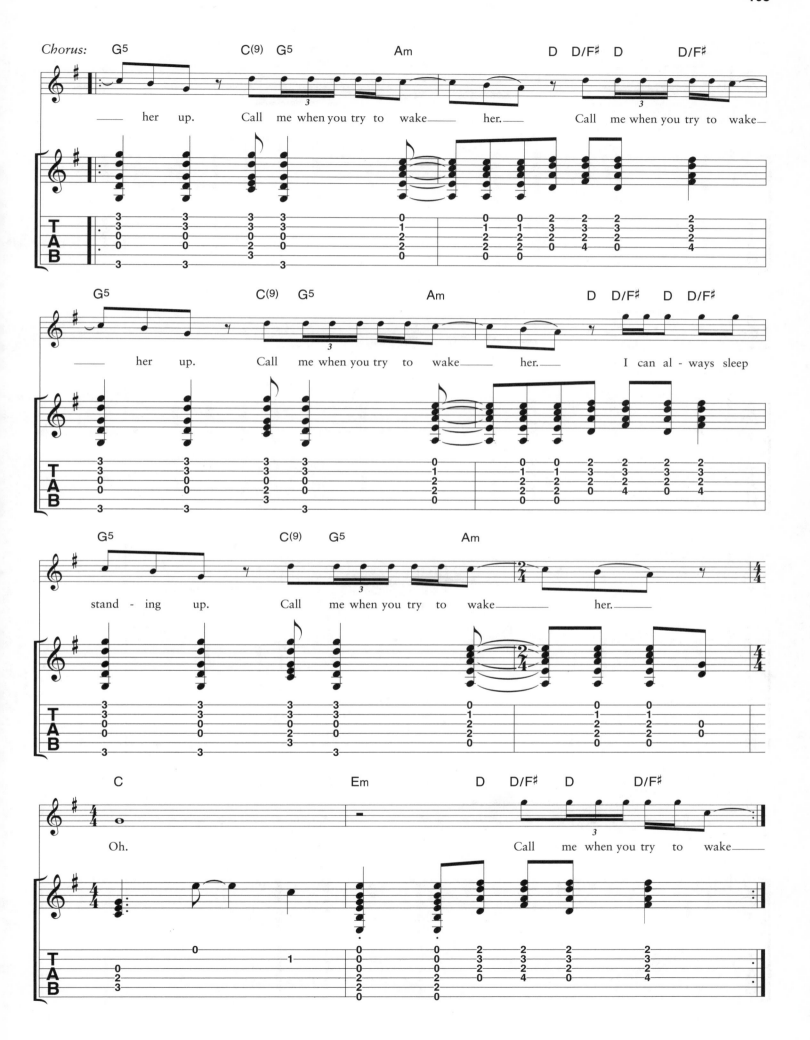

STAND

Words and Music by William Berry, Peter Buck, Michael Mills and Michael Stipe

110

Electrolite

Words and Music by William Berry, Peter Buck, Michael Mills and Michael Stipe

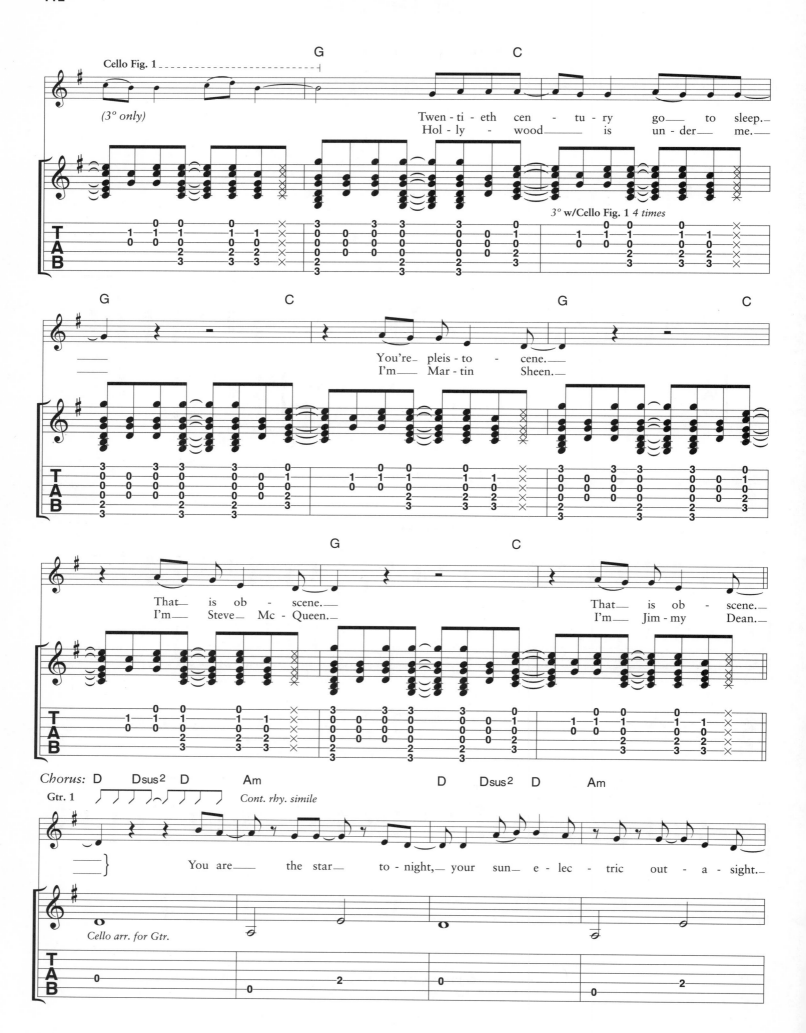

114

Verse 3:
If you ever want to fly
Mulholland Drive.
Up in the sky.
Stand on a cliff and look down there.
Don't be scared.
You are alive.
You are alive.

You are the star *etc.*

ALL THE RIGHT FRIENDS

Words and Music by William Berry, Peter Buck, Michael Mills and Michael Stipe

Backing Vocal Fig. 1

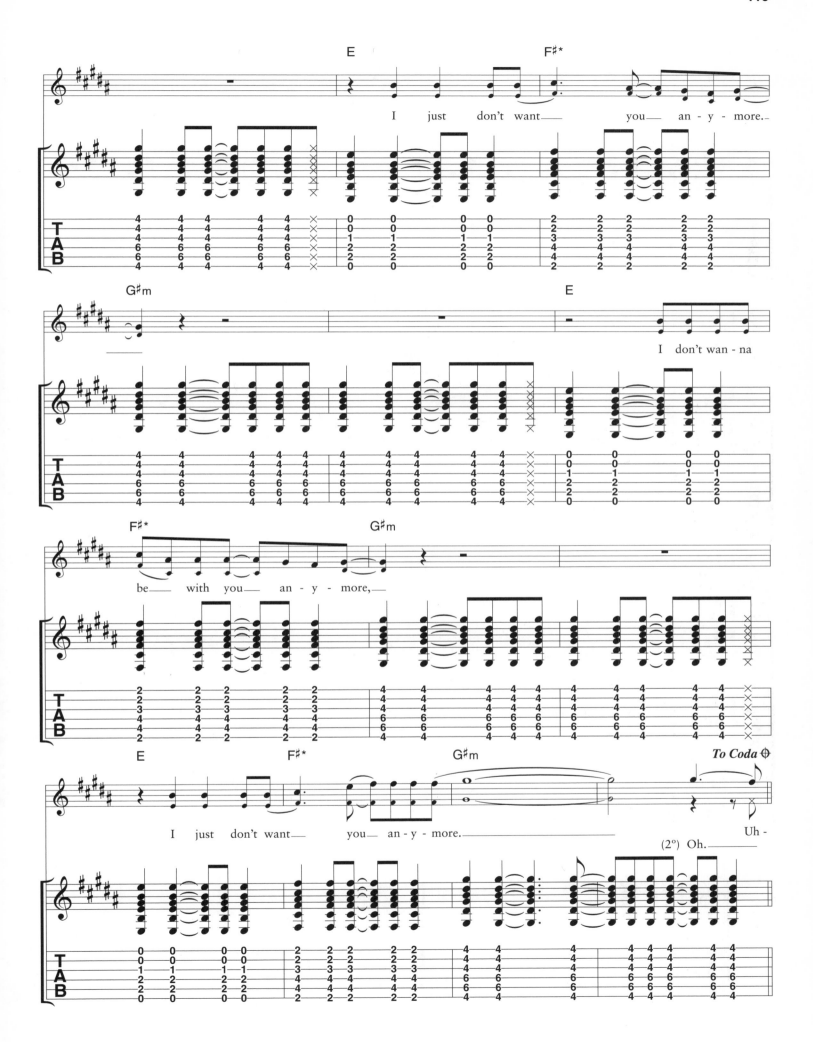

EVERYBODY HURTS

Words and Music by William Berry, Peter Buck, Michael Mills and Michael Stipe

AT MY MOST BEAUTIFUL

Words and Music by Peter Buck, Michael Mills and Michael Stipe

© 1998 Temporary Music, USA

Warner/Chappell North America Ltd, London W6 8BS

NIGHTSWIMMING

Words and Music by William Berry, Peter Buck, Michael Mills and Michael Stipe